Eli Manning

Revised Edition

By Jeff Savage

AMAZING ATHLETES

Lerner Publications Company • Minneapolis

Lerner Publications Company
A division of Lerner Publishing Group, Inc.
241 First Avenue North
Minneapolis, MN 55401 U.S.A.

Website address: www.lernerbooks.com

Library of Congress Cataloging-in-Publication Data

Savage, Jeff, 1961–
    Eli Manning / by Jeff Savage. — Rev. ed.
        p.   cm.— (Amazing athletes)
    Includes index.
    ISBN 978–1–4677–0873–9 (lib. bdg.: alk. paper)
    1. Manning, Eli, 1981–—Juvenile literature. 2. Football players—United States—Biography—Juvenile literature. 3. Quarterbacks (Football)—United States—Biography—Juvenile literature. I. Title.
GV939.M2887S28 2013
796.332092—dc23 [B]   2012001248

Manufactured in the United States of America
1 – BP – 7/15/12

TABLE OF CONTENTS

Eli throws a pass against the New England Patriots.

THE BIG GAME

New York Giants **quarterback** Eli Manning looked at the clock. Less than four minutes were left in the 2012 **Super Bowl**. The Giants trailed the New England Patriots, 17–15.

Thousands of fans shouted from their seats.

Millions more were watching on TV. But Eli stayed calm. He knew what to do. Eli had led the Giants to victory in the 2008 Super Bowl.

With his team down by two points, Eli and the Giants would only need a **field goal** to go ahead of the Patriots. But Eli wanted a **touchdown** to take an even bigger lead.

Eli launched a pass deep down the left side of the field. Giants **wide receiver** Mario Manningham was there. He reached up between two **defenders** and caught the ball.

Fans cheer on the Giants during the 2012 Super Bowl.

Mario Manningham catches the ball between two defenders during the fourth quarter.

It was a big play. But New York still had 50 yards to go for a touchdown.

Eli threw more passes to Manningham and Hakeem Nicks. The ball was at the six-yard line with just over a minute to go. New York **running back** Ahmad Bradshaw ran up the middle. The Patriots let him get into the **end zone** for a touchdown! New England let the Giants score so New England could get the ball back with time still on the clock.

The Patriots got the ball with 57 seconds left in the game. They trailed the Giants, 21–17. But New England and star quarterback Tom Brady ran out of time. The Giants were Super Bowl champions for the second time in five years!

Eli was named Most Valuable Player (MVP) of the Super Bowl for the second time. But the star quarterback knows that he can't win by himself. "This isn't about one person," Eli said. "This is about a team coming together."

Eli holds up the Super Bowl trophy after beating the Patriots.

Left to right: Peyton, Eli, and Cooper Manning wear jerseys in honor of their father. He had worn number 18 as quarterback at Ole Miss.

The Quiet Brother

Elisha Nelson Manning was born January 3, 1981, in New Orleans, Louisiana. Eli was the youngest son of Archie and Olivia Manning. Archie had been the star quarterback at the University of Mississippi (nicknamed Ole Miss), where he met Olivia. He also played for 14 years in the NFL, mostly for the New Orleans Saints. Eli's oldest brother, Cooper, played wide receiver in high school before a spinal problem cut short his career. Peyton, the next oldest, was the quarterback for the Indianapolis Colts for 14 seasons. Naturally, Eli followed his father and brothers to the football field.

Peyton and Cooper were competitive growing up. Eli was quiet and shy. He liked to spend time with his mother. Archie often took the two older boys to sporting events. Olivia took Eli shopping. Peyton liked to pick on Eli. Cooper protected him.

Eli struggled to learn to read. He almost had to repeat the first grade. His parents switched him from Isidore Newman School, where his brothers went, to a smaller school. Eli's friends teased him. He worked hard to improve so he

Eli grew up in New Orleans, Louisiana.

could return to Newman. Eli rejoined Isidore Newman for eighth grade.

Eli was an outstanding athlete. But he was always humble. "Eli would come home from one of his baseball games and not say a word, and you'd ask him how it went," said his brother Cooper. "He'd say 'Good,' and not much more. We'd later find out that he'd hit a game-winning homer in the bottom of the ninth inning. If it was Peyton in the same situation, he'd barge through the front door and yell." Eli was more calm and laid back than his brothers. He earned the nickname Easy.

Eli's nickname is Easy because he is easygoing. On the football field, he stays calm in a crisis. "When things are going bad, I've got to settle everyone down," Eli says. "I have to be the leader of the team."

Newman High School coach Frank Gendusa talks to Eli before a game.

Eli played quarterback for his school's **varsity** team for three years, just like Peyton before him. Eli threw for at least 2,000 yards and 20 touchdowns all three seasons. He finished his high school career with almost 200 more yards passing than Peyton. Dozens of colleges **recruited** Eli to play football for them. He chose his dad's former school, Ole Miss.

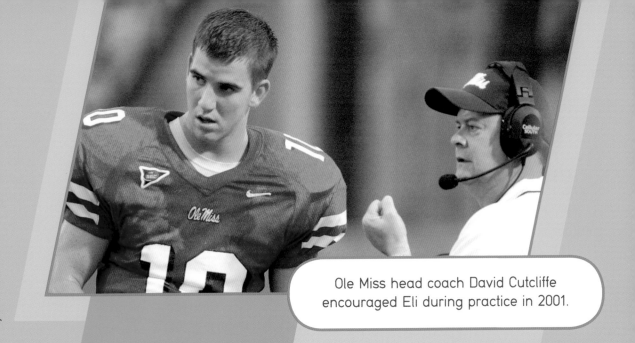

Ole Miss head coach David Cutcliffe encouraged Eli during practice in 2001.

OLE MISS

Eli was a star at Ole Miss—but not at first. In 1999, he was **redshirted.** In 2000, he was a backup. In the fourth quarter of that season's final game—the Music City Bowl against West Virginia—he finally got a chance to play. He completed 12 of 20 passes for 167 yards and three touchdowns! Eli proved he was ready to lead the Ole Miss Rebels.

Eli guided Mississippi to a 6–1 record to start the 2001 season. Then, against Arkansas, he threw for 312 yards and six touchdowns. But the Rebels lost that game in seven **overtimes**, 58–56. In 2002, Eli led the Rebels to the Independence Bowl. They won 27–23 over Nebraska. But Eli saved his best for 2003. He led Ole Miss to a 10-win season, which included a 31–28 triumph over Oklahoma State in the Cotton Bowl.

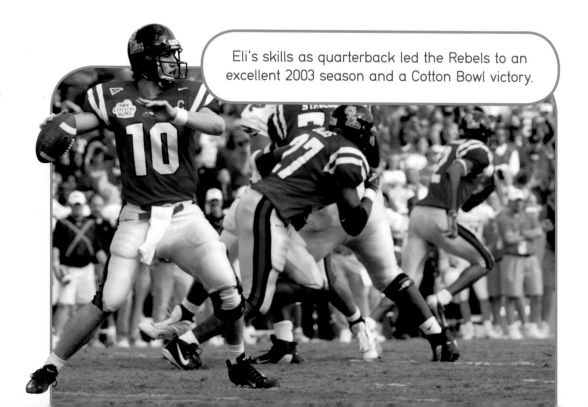

Eli's skills as quarterback led the Rebels to an excellent 2003 season and a Cotton Bowl victory.

Eli had set 47 passing records at Ole Miss. His play won him many honors, including the Maxwell Award as the nation's best all-around player.

Eli won the Maxwell Award in 2003.

Eli entered the NFL **Draft** in 2004. He seemed likely to be an NFL star. After all, Peyton had become a star for the Colts, and Archie was ready to offer guidance anytime.

The San Diego Chargers held the top pick in the draft. They had long been a losing team. They needed a quarterback. But Eli and his father made it clear that he did not want to play for the Chargers. San Diego chose Eli with the first pick anyway. Eli was heartbroken. He talked about quitting football.

Three picks later, the New York Giants chose quarterback Philip Rivers. Then came word of a trade. The Chargers traded Eli to the Giants for Rivers and three picks in the 2005 draft. The entire Manning family was thrilled. But Eli would have to show he was worth the trade.

Eli's family supported him at the 2004 NFL Draft. *From left*: Peyton and his wife, Ashley; Olivia; Eli's girlfriend (now wife), Abby McGrew; Eli; and Archie.

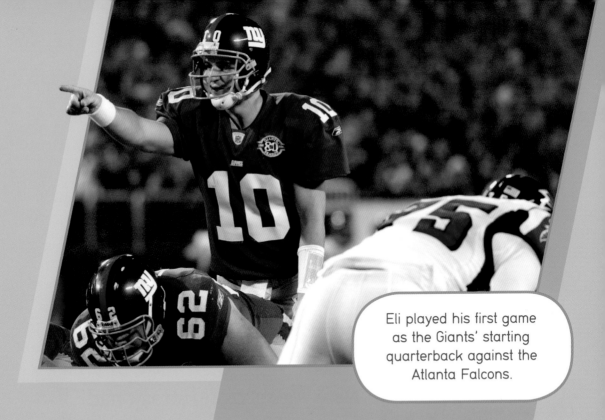

Eli played his first game as the Giants' starting quarterback against the Atlanta Falcons.

FINDING HIS WAY

Eli struggled as a **rookie**. The Giants plodded through the first half of the 2004–2005 season with **veteran** Kurt Warner playing quarterback. Eli mostly watched from the sidelines. Midway through the year, coach Tom Coughlin decided to try Eli as his starting player.

A football game is like a three-hour test. Before taking the test, Eli has to prepare. He studies films, goes to practice, and lifts weights. These efforts help him improve his play during the three hours he's on the field.

Eli threw his first NFL touchdown pass against the Atlanta Falcons. But he also threw two **interceptions**. The Giants lost that game and the next three. Against the Baltimore Ravens, Eli completed only four passes. New York's losing streak had reached eight games when the Giants faced the Dallas Cowboys in the season's final game. Eli led the offense on a last-minute touchdown drive to win, 28–24. Eli had shown a spark.

Eli worked hard in the off-season. He lifted weights. He studied the **playbook**. He watched **game film**. In 2005, the Giants officially named Eli the starting quarterback. He was ready. He led the team to victories over the Arizona Cardinals and the New Orleans Saints. Next, the Giants traveled to San Diego to play the Chargers.

San Diego fans had not forgotten that Eli had snubbed their team on draft day. They booed loudly every time he touched the ball. Eli stayed calm. He played his best game yet as a pro, passing for 352 yards and two touchdowns. But the Giants could not stop San Diego running back LaDainian Tomlinson. New York lost, 45–23.

San Diego Chargers fans were still upset that Eli had snubbed their team during the draft.

Eli played well in 2005. But the team had some disappointing losses.

The Giants returned home to face the St. Louis Rams. Eli torched the Rams' defense with four touchdown passes in a 44–24 victory.

Two games later, he led the offense on a last-minute drive against the Denver Broncos. Eli threw a touchdown strike to Amani Toomer with five seconds left. The Giants won, 24–23.

The Giants finished with an 11–5 record to make the playoffs.

Eli was near the top of the league in passing yards and touchdowns. Unfortunately, he also threw 17 interceptions and completed barely half his passes. Worse yet, he threw three more interceptions at home against the Carolina Panthers in the first round of the playoffs. The Giants lost, 23–0. They became the first playoff team in 25 years to go scoreless at home.

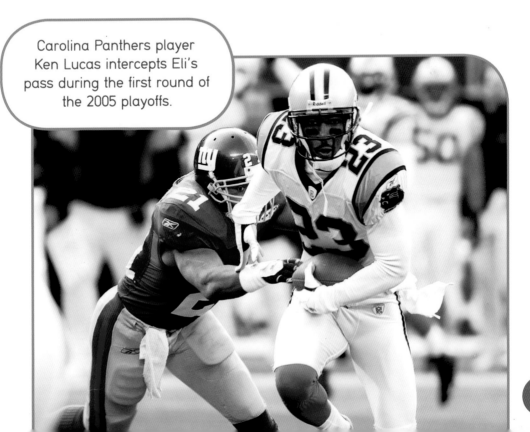

Carolina Panthers player Ken Lucas intercepts Eli's pass during the first round of the 2005 playoffs.

Eli *(left)* congratulates his brother Peyton *(right)* after Peyton's Colts beat the Giants during the 2006–2007 season.

ONE GIANT LEAP

Giants fans were unhappy. They expected more from Eli. Newspaper reporters wrote negative stories about him.

Eli didn't get upset. He calmly led New York to a 6–2 record to start the 2006–2007 season. Then injuries hit. Several Giants couldn't play. The losses piled up. New York finished the season with an 8–8 record. They barely made the playoffs and lost again in the first round.

Success in 2007–2008 seemed unlikely. The team had many injuries. Star running back Tiki Barber retired. Fans and players wondered if Eli was up to the job.

The Giants fought hard all season. They won three of their final five games to earn another trip to the playoffs. This time, the Giants took control. They beat the Tampa Bay Buccaneers, the Dallas Cowboys, and the Green Bay Packers.

Eli throws a pass against Tampa Bay.

The Giants were headed to the Super Bowl to take on the New England Patriots!

In the 2008 Super Bowl, the Patriots took a 7–3 lead on the first play of the second quarter. Neither team scored again until the fourth quarter. Eli threw a touchdown pass to David Tyree with 11:05 left.

Patriots quarterback Tom Brady drove his team 80 yards to the end zone to retake the

Eli breaks free of the Patriots' defense to throw a pass.

Eli *(right)* holds the Super Bowl trophy during a parade in New York.

lead, 14–10. Once more, the pressure was on Eli. He swiftly moved his team down the field. At the 13-yard line, the Patriots **blitzed**. Eli lofted a perfect pass. Wide receiver Plaxico Burress caught the pass for the winning touchdown! New York won, 17–14. The Giants were Super Bowl champions. Eli was named MVP of the game.

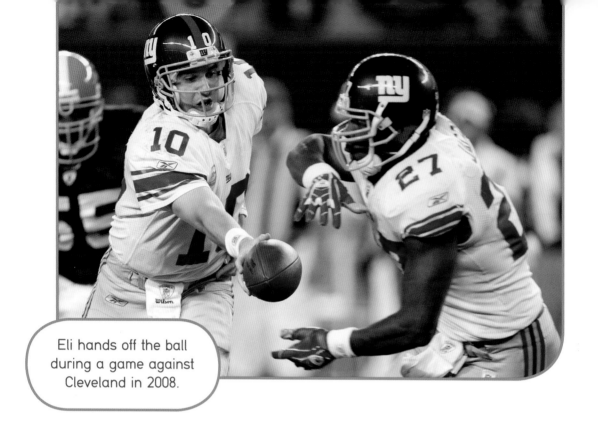

Eli hands off the ball during a game against Cleveland in 2008.

The Giants believed in themselves. They knew that they could succeed if they played as a team. "We shocked the world but not ourselves," said Giants defender Antonio Pierce after the big game.

Eli married his college girlfriend, Abby McGrew, in 2008.

The Giants only lost four games during the 2008–2009 season. But they lost to the Philadelphia Eagles in the second round of the playoffs. The Giants missed the playoffs in both the 2009–2010 and 2010–2011 seasons. In 2011–2012, the Giants won nine games in the regular season. Then they tore through the playoffs and beat the Patriots in the Super Bowl for the second time.

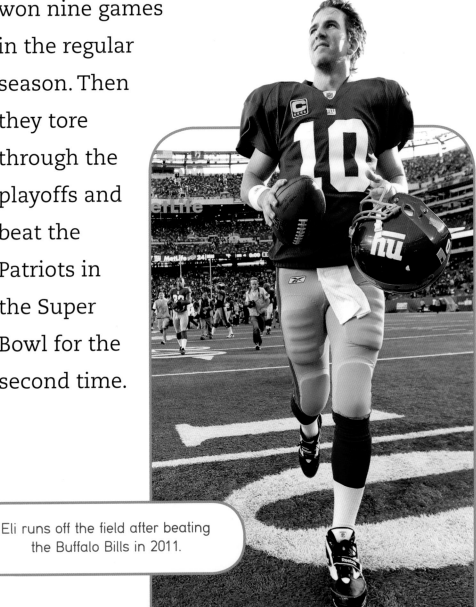

Eli runs off the field after beating the Buffalo Bills in 2011.

Eli had proved his doubters wrong many times. After winning the Super Bowl in 2008, Eli said he often wondered if he deserved all the criticism he received. When he won the big game again in 2012, Eli wasn't in the mood to think about the past. "It just feels good to win a Super Bowl," he said.

Eli *(right)* performs on *Saturday Night Live* in 2012.

Selected Career Highlights

2011–2012   Named Super Bowl Most Valuable Player for the second time
Led New York Giants to the Super Bowl title for the second time
Named to Pro Bowl for the second time

2010–2011   Set career high with 31 touchdown passes

2009–2010   Set career high with 4,021 yards passing

2008–2009   Named to Pro Bowl for the first time

2007–2008   Named Super Bowl Most Valuable Player
Led New York Giants to the Super Bowl title
Led Giants to a NFC record three straight playoff road victories

2006–2007   Threw 24 touchdown passes

2005–2006   Passed for 3,762 yards and 24 touchdowns
Led Giants to 11–5 record and NFC East title

2004–2005   Selected first in the NFL Draft
Made NFL debut against Philadelphia Eagles, completing three
of nine passes for 66 yards

2003   Won Johnny Unitas Golden Arm Award as top college
quarterback
Won Walter Camp Football Foundation Player of the Year Award
Named First Team All-America
Named Southeastern Conference Player of the
Year

2002   Named to the Southeastern
Conference Academic Honor Roll

2001   Named to the Southeastern Conference
Academic Honor Roll
Won Conerly Trophy as Best College
Football Player in Mississippi

2000   Named to the Southeastern Conference
Academic Honor Roll

1998   Named to High School All-America team
Named *USA Today* State Player of
the Year in Louisiana

Glossary

blitzed: sent extra defensive players to rush the quarterback

defenders: players whose job it is to try to stop the other team from scoring points

draft: a yearly event in which professional teams take turns choosing new players from a selected group

end zone: the area beyond the goal line at either end of the field. To score, a team tries to get the ball into the other team's end zone.

field goal: a successful kick over the U-shaped upright poles. A field goal is worth three points.

game film: videotape of a game that players and coaches study

interceptions: passes caught by a player on the defense. An interception results in the opposing team getting control of the ball.

overtimes: extra periods of play to break a tie. In college football, each team is given one possession to score. If both teams score an equal number of points, another overtime is played. In pro football, the first team to score wins.

playbook: descriptions of a team's offensive and defensive plays

quarterback: the person who throws or hands off the ball

recruited: offered a chance to play on a team by a scout searching for players

redshirted: made to sit out for the first year on a college team to learn. A player starts his college career in the second year and is still allowed to play for four years.

rookie: a first-year player

running back: a football player whose main job is to run with the ball

Super Bowl: the final game of each season between the champions of the American Football Conference and the National Football Conference. The winner of the Super Bowl is that season's NFL champion.

touchdown: a six-point score. A team scores a touchdown when it gets into the other team's end zone with the ball.

varsity: the top level in ability of a school team, above the junior varsity and freshman teams

veteran: a player with two or more years of experience

wide receiver: a player who catches passes, mainly for a big gain

Further Reading & Websites

Kennedy, Mike, and Mark Stewart. *Touchdown: The Power and Precision of Football's Perfect Play*. Minneapolis: Millbrook Press, 2010.

Savage, Jeff. *Peyton Manning* Rev. ed. Minneapolis: Lerner Publications Company, 2013.

Savage, Jeff. *Tom Brady*. Rev. ed. Minneapolis: Lerner Publications Company, 2009.

Official NFL Site
http://www.nfl.com
The official National Football League website provides fans with game action, statistics, schedules, and biographies of players.

The Official Site of the New York Giants
http://www.giants.com
The official website of the New York Giants includes the team schedule and game results, late-breaking news, biographies of Eli Manning and other players and coaches, and much more.

Sports Illustrated Kids
http://www.sikids.com
The *Sports Illustrated Kids* website covers all sports, including football.

Index

Photo Acknowledgments

The images in this book are used with the permission of: © Jim Davis/The Boston Globe via Getty Images, p. 4; © Ezra Shaw/Getty Images, p. 5; © Sam Riche/MCT via Getty Images, p. 6; © Al Bello/Getty Images, p. 7; © Michael C. Herbert/US Presswire, p. 8; © Prisma/SuperStock, p. 10; AP Photo/David Rae Morris, p. 12; AP Photo/Rogelio Solis, p. 13; © Ronald Martinez/Getty Images, p. 14; AP Photo/Scott Audette, p. 15; © Chris Trotman/Getty Images, p. 16; John Angelillo/UPI/Newscom, p. 17; © Stephen Dunn/Getty Images, p. 19; AP Photo/Kathy Willens, p. 20; © Tom Berg/NFL/Getty Images, p. 21; © Travis Lindquist/Getty Images, p. 22; AP Photo/Steve Nesius, p. 23; © Andy Lyons/Getty Images, p. 24; AP Photo/Frank Franklin II, p. 25; © Gregory Shamus/Getty Images, p. 26; © Chris Trotman/Getty Images, p. 27; © Dana Edelson/NBC/NBCU Photo Bank/Getty Images, p. 28; AP Photo/Paul Jasienski, p. 29.

Front cover: AP Photo/Evan Pinkus.

Main body text set in Caecilia LT Std 55 Roman 16/28.
Typeface provided by Adobe Systems.